AMAZING ANIMAL BODIES

HORNS AND ANTLERS

ANNE ACCARDI

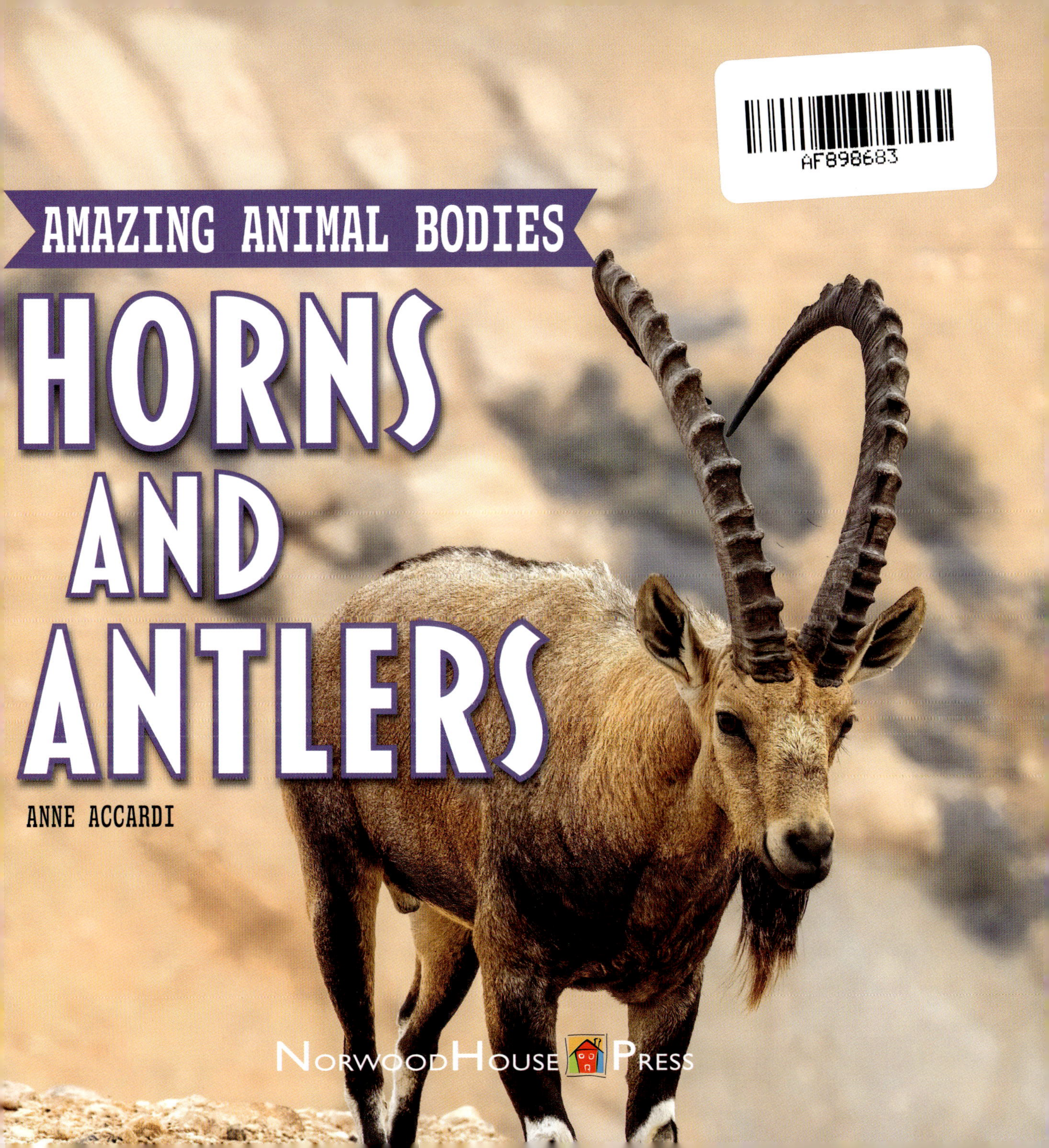

NorwoodHouse Press

Cataloging-in-Publication Data

Names: Accardi, Anne.
Title: Horns and antlers / Anne Accardi.
Description: Buffalo, NY : Norwood House Press, 2027. | Series: Amazing animal bodies | Includes glossary and index.
Identifiers: ISBN 9781978579545 (pbk.) | ISBN 9781978579552 (library bound) | ISBN 9781978579569 (ebook)
Subjects: LCSH: Horns--Juvenile literature. | Antlers--Juvenile literature.
Classification: LCC QL942.A33 2027 | DDC 591.47--dc23

Published in 2027 by
Norwood House Press
2544 Clinton Street
Buffalo, NY 14224

Designer: Rhea Magaro
Editor: Kim Thompson

Photo credits: Cover, p. 1 Luciano Santandreu/Shutterstock.com; p. 5 KennethHK/Shutterstock.com; p. 6 Sergej Razvodovskij/Shutterstock.com; p. 7 Giedriius/Shutterstock.com; p. 8 Bangkit's Galery/Shutterstock.com; p. 9 Number One/Shutterstock.com; p. 11 Tom Havranek/Shutterstock.com; p. 13 JacobLoyacano/Shutterstock.com; p. 14 Harry Collins Photography/Shutterstock.com; p. 17 smereka/Shutterstock.com; p. 18 Henk Bogaard/Shutterstock.com; p. 19 Stacey Newman/Shutterstock.com; p. 20 Tanmoy_Adhikary/ Shutterstock.com;

Printed in the United States of America

CPSIA compliance information: Batch #CSNHP27: For further information contact Norwood House Press at 1-800-237-9932.

TABLE OF CONTENTS

What Are Horns and Antlers?

Horns and antlers are body parts. They grow on some animals' heads.

Usually, only males have antlers. Males and females have horns.

Antlers are **bones**. They **branch** out.

They get **shed** once a year.

New antlers grow. **Velvet** covers them as they grow. Then, the velvet rubs off.

Horns are made of bone and **keratin**.

Horns do not shed. They keep growing.

Deer Antlers

Male deer are called bucks. Bucks use antlers to **attract** mates.

Moose Antlers

Male moose are called bulls. Their antlers are huge! Bulls use antlers to fight off wolves and bears.

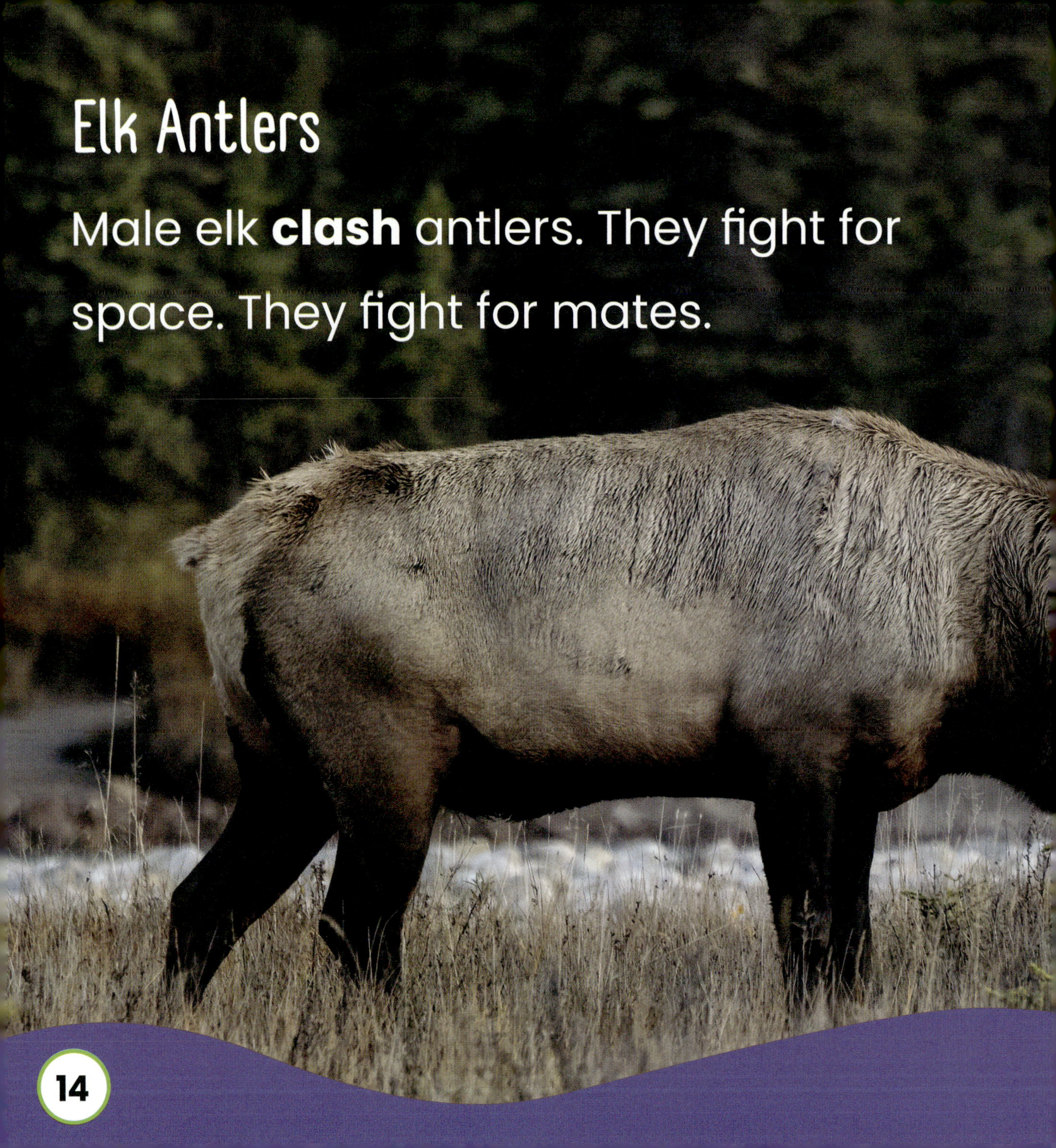

Elk Antlers

Male elk **clash** antlers. They fight for space. They fight for mates.

Cow Horns

Cow horns can be short or long. Some are straight. Some curl.

Big horns warn other cows to stay away!

Rhino Horns

Rhinos have one or two horns. They use their horns to protect babies.

Rhinos scratch trees with their horns. This marks their space.

Goat Horns

Some goat horns curve. Some twist.

Goats **butt** heads. They fight with their horns. This shows who is in charge.

Glossary

attract (uh-TRAKT): to interest; to make someone like you or want to come closer

bones (bohnz): the hard, white body parts that make up the skeleton of a person or an animal

branch (branch): to divide into parts that go in different directions

butt (but): to hit with the head

clash (klash): to strike two things against each other

keratin (KER-uh-tin): the natural material that makes up hair and fingernails and that is found in animal horns

shed (shed): to drop off naturally; to fall off

velvet (VEL-vit): the soft skin that covers an animal's antlers while they are growing

Thinking Questions

1. What is the difference between antlers and horns?

2. What is velvet?

3. Why do animals use antlers and horns to fight each other?

4. How do animals use antlers and horns to protect themselves?

5. Describe cow horns.

Index

About the Author

Anne Accardi is a librarian who loves reading books and learning new things! She lives in Kansas City, Missouri. When she's not writing, Anne enjoys listening to music, exploring nature around the city, and spending time with her family.